There's a monster in the tree, in the tree.
There's a monster in the tree, in the tree.

There's a monster in the tree,
And he's counting up to three.
There's a monster in the tree,
in the tree.

There's a monster at the door, at the door.
4　**There's a monster at the door, at the door.**

There's a monster at the door,
And she's dancing on the floor.
There's a monster at the door,
at the door.

There's a monster in the hall,
in the hall.
There's a monster in the hall,
in the hall.

There's a monster in the hall,
And he's playing with a ball.
There's a monster in the hall,
in the hall.

There's a monster in the kitchen,
in the kitchen.
There's a monster in the kitchen,
in the kitchen.

8

There's a monster in the kitchen,
And she's singing with a chicken.
There's a monster in the kitchen,
in the kitchen.

9

There's a monster in the pot,
in the pot.
There's a monster in the pot,
in the pot.

There's a monster in the pot,
And he's getting very hot.
There's a monster in the pot,
in the pot.

There's a monster in the bedroom, in the bedroom.
There's a monster in the bedroom, in the bedroom.

12

There's a monster in the bedroom,
And she's sweeping with a red broom.
There's a monster in the bedroom,
in the bedroom.

There are monsters in the bed, in the bed.

14 **There are monsters in the bed, in the bed.**

There are monsters in the bed,
"Good-night" is what they said.
There are monsters in the bed, in the bed.

"Good night!"